Contents

Animal habitats

Where do different animals make their homes?

Animals live in places where they can find food. Some animals live by the sea so they can catch fish. This is called their **habitat**.

KINGFISHER READERS

Where Animals Live

Brenda Stones

First published 2012 by Kingfisher
an imprint of Macmillan Children's Books
a division of Macmillan Publishers Limited
20 New Wharf Road, London N1 9RR
Basingstoke and Oxford
Associated companies throughout the world
www.panmacmillan.com

Series editor: Heather Morris
Literacy consultant: Hilary Horton

ISBN: 978-0-7534-3053-8

9 8 7 6 5 4 3 2

2TR/1011/WKT/UNTD/105MA

A CIP catalogue record for this book is available from the British Library.

Printed in China

Picture credits
The Publisher would like to thank the following for permission to reproduce their material. Every care has been taken to trace copyright holders. However, if there have been unintentional omissions or failure to trac copyright holders, we apologise and will, if informed, endeavour to make corrections in any future edition.
Top = t; Bottom = b; Centre = c; Left = l; Right = r
Cover Shutterstock (SS)/RCPPHOTO; Pages 4 SS/Pichuigin Dmitry; 5t SS/Jill Battglio; 5b SS/Hannamariah; 6–7 Photolibrary; 7 FLPA/Yva Momatiuk & John Eastcott; 8 SS/Nik Nikiz; 9 FLPA/ZSSD/Minden; 10 FLPA/Panada Photo; 11 SS/Vladimir Chernyansky; 12–13 SS/MTrebbin; 13t SS/Tramper; 14–15 SS/alterfalter; 15 SS/Kristof Degreef; 16 SS/Robert Hackett; 17t SS/Anne Kitzman; 17b FLPA/Imagebroker; 18t SS/Johan Sanepoel; 18b SS/Four Oaks; 19 SS/Joy Brown; 20 Nature PL/Kim Taylor; 21 SS/Krisvosheev Vitaly; 22 SS/Mikhail Olykainan; 23 Alamy/Chris Howes; 24 SS/janr34; 25t SS/Studiotouch; 25b SS/Indric; 26–27 Photolibrary; 27 SS/Cathy Keifer; 28 Photolibrary; 29 Photolibrary/Usher D; 30 SS/Graham Taylor; 31t Alamy/Kevin Foy; 31b SS/RCPPHOTO.

Many animals build homes to protect their young. Some animals build nests in trees. Others dig **burrows** or **dens** underground.

Penguins

Most penguins live near the South Pole. They live in large groups, called **colonies**. For most of the year the penguins move around to find fish to eat.

When penguins are ready to lay eggs, they settle down near the sea. In the emperor penguin family, the father penguin keeps the egg warm on his feet until it hatches.

Polar bears

Polar bears live near the North Pole. They live on the **sea ice**, where they hunt seals and fish.

When the mother bear is ready to have **cubs**, she digs a den in the snow. The den keeps the cubs warm from November to March.

Foxes

Most foxes live in fields and woods, but some now find more food in towns. Foxes mainly hunt at night and sleep in the day.

n the fields, the fox digs a den in
he ground. In the town, the fox
night dig a hole under a garden
hed and use it as a den.

Moles

Moles live underground in fields and gardens. Moles are hard to spot but molehills show where they have been. Molehills are piles of soil that moles throw up when they dig tunnels.

The mole's underground home is called a burrow. The mole digs its burrow with its long claws and sharp teeth.

Chimpanzees

Chimpanzees live in forests in Africa. Their long arms help them swing from the trees.

Chimpanzees sleep in nests in trees. They build a new nest every night.

Chimps live with lots of families in a colony. The baby chimp keeps close to its mother for three or four years.

Squirrels

Most squirrels live in trees, in woodlands, parks and gardens.

Squirrels use their sharp claws to climb and jump between trees. They use their tail to balance.

The squirrel builds a nest called a **drey**. It is made of twigs and leaves, with piles of warm moss inside.

These baby squirrels are in a drey.

Building nests

Many birds build nests to protect their eggs. These amazing nests are made by the weaver bird. It weaves them from thin bits of leaf.

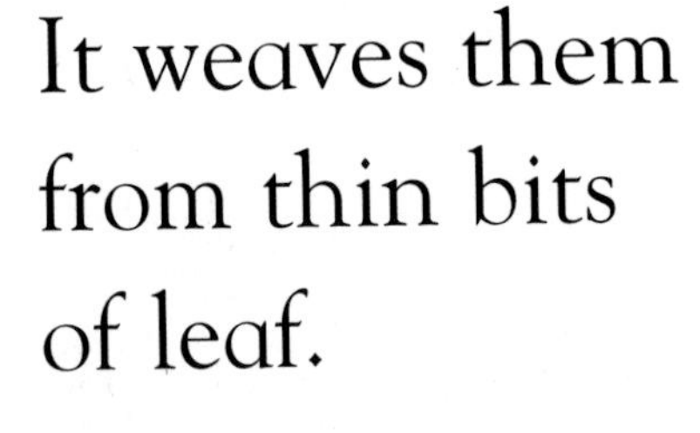

Here is a swan's nest. The mother swan sits on her eggs for 40 days. The father swan will scare away other birds or dogs.

Swallows

The swallow has more than one home. It spends the summer in one place and then flies away to somewhere warm for the winter. This is called **migration**.

The swallow always comes back to the same place each summer.

It builds its nest under the roof of a house with mud and twigs. When it comes back, it only has to make a few repairs!

Ants

Ants are very small, but they put a lot of work into building their homes. Just look at this **anthill**!

Ants work together as a team. They carry sticks and leaves to build their home.

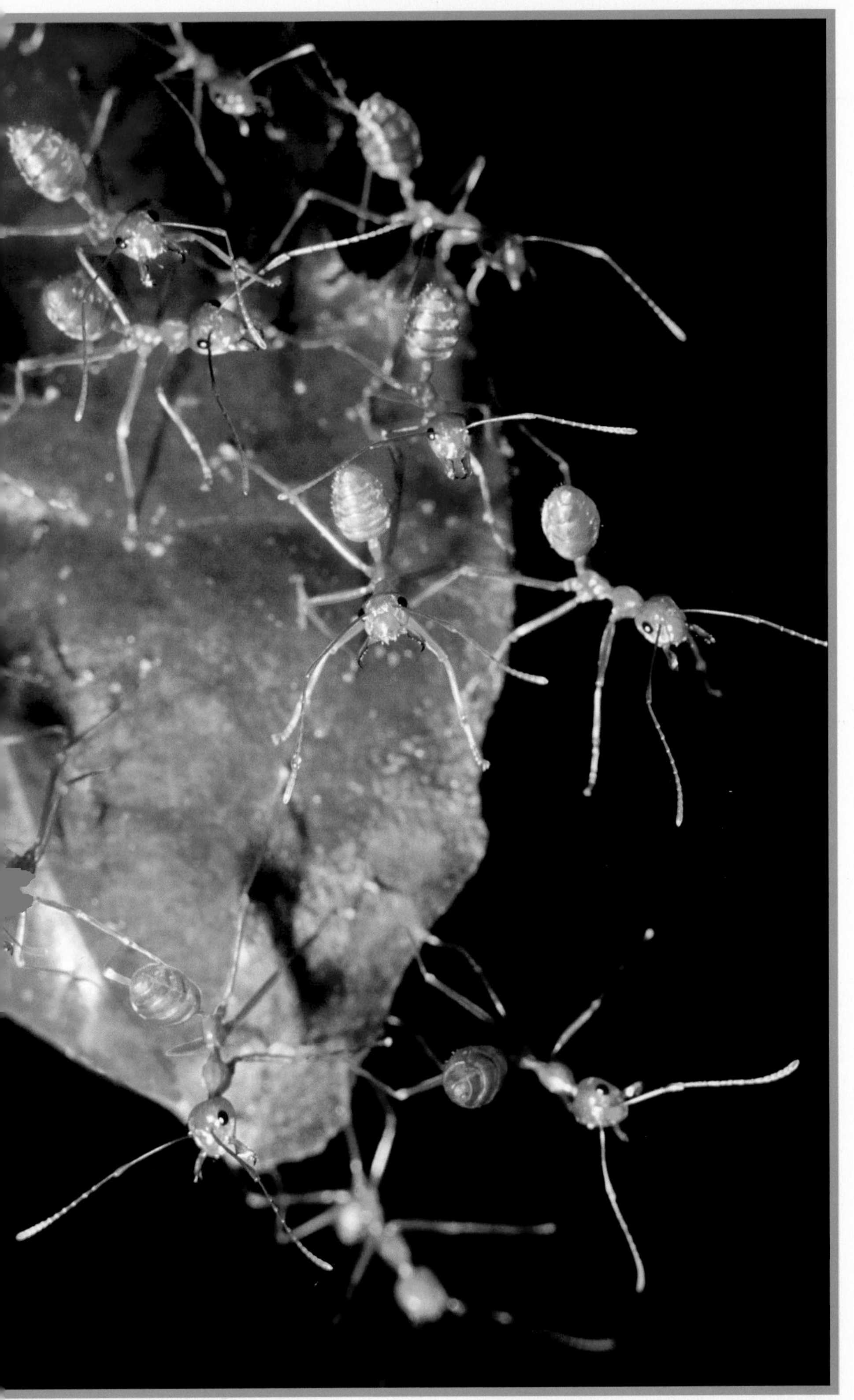

Wasps

Wasps also work as a team. They build these amazing nests in trees, or in holes in walls.

Wasps make their nests from chewed bits of wood. The nests look like paper.

n each colony of wasps there is
one queen wasp who lays the eggs.

All the other wasps build the nest
and find the food.

Butterflies

Butterflies live in fields and gardens, where they feed on plants.

There are many kinds of butterfly. Each kind chooses a plant that is the right colour or taste for them.

Γhe butterfly lays its eggs on the eaf of the plant. When the eggs ıatch they become caterpillars. Γhe caterpillars eat the leaf.

Spiders

Spiders live in every kind of habitat. You can find them in houses, in parks and in woods. Spiders spin webs to catch their food.

Some spiders spin a nest that looks like a soft, white ball.

Changing habitats

What animal habitats have we seen? We have looked at sea and ice, forests and fields.

What animal homes have we seen? We have looked at dens, burrows and nests.

But habitats are changing. Ice is melting and people are cutting down forests.

We must try to protect habitats so that animals like the giant panda don't lose their homes.

Glossary

anthill the home that ants build

burrow the underground home of rabbits and moles

colony a group of animal families, like penguins, chimpanzees or wasps

cub a baby bear or fox

den the underground home of bears and foxes

drey the treetop home of a squirrel

habitat the kind of place where an animal lives

migration when birds fly away for part of the year

molehill the earth thrown up by a burrowing mole

sea ice the cold habitat of polar bears